Eastern Thinking

~ for a ~

Western World

A Dialog on Tai Chi with
Master Arthur Rosenfeld

Edited and Published by:

Tim Johnson

- and -

The Martial Arts Lineage Project

ISBN-13: 978-1479166350

ISBN-10: 1479166359

www.MALineage.com

Introduction

This book is derived from a a dialog with Master Arthur Rosenfeld that took place in November of 2011. As part of the Martial Arts Lineage Project, this discussion revolves around the development of Chen-Style Tai Chi as it has evolved from Eastern cultures into the West and offered its benefits to a society in need of philosophical, medical, and spiritual guidance. Master Rosenfeld shares lessons he has learned along the path of his life and offers insights into the historical development of tai chi as a battlefield art built on a tripod of Chinese medicine, body mechanics, and Taoist philosophy.

It is with great pleasure that I bring you this discourse—which I am sure you will thoroughly enjoy—with the brilliant and insightful Master Arthur Rosenfeld.

About Master Arthur Rosenfeld

Master Arthur Rosenfeld is a contributor to national magazines such as *Vogue*, *Vanity Fair*, and *Parade*. He has been seen on Fox News and other networks, and has been heard on numerous national radio programs. He also hosts the hit national PBS television show *Longevity tai chi with Arthur Rosenfeld.*

Master Rosenfeld began his formal martial arts training in 1980 and has both a strong reputation in the industry and an august martial lineage. As a Yale graduate, he combines the scientific background and communication skills gained through post-graduate studies at Cornell and the University of California with real-world experience in creative, high-level corporate positions.

A prolific author, Master Rosenfeld has published both fiction and non-fiction books, including martial arts thrillers he describes as "Kung Fu Noir". His bestselling title *The Truth*

About Chronic Pain (Basic Books, New York, May 2003) was a finalist for the "Books for a Better Life" award alongside a work by the Dalai Lama. His book *Tai Chi — The Perfect Exercise*, will be released in April of 2013.

In 2011 Master Rosenfeld was the recipient of the World Qigong Congress Tai Chi Master of the Year Award. In 2012, he was the recipient of the Action on Film Festival Maverick Award for outstanding contributions to martial arts in the media. Previous recipients of this award include Diana Lee Inosanto, John Savage, Talia Shire, and David Carradine.

He is the first Westerner to be ordained a monk at the Chun Yang (Pure Yang) Taoist monastery in Guangzhou, China. For more information about Master Arthur Rosenfeld, visit his website: www.arthurrosenfeld.com

"Our goal is to just to keep
our own equilibrium."

~ *Master Arthur Rosenfeld*

A Dialog on Tai Chi with Master Arthur Rosenfeld

Tim: As we are martial artists raised in the West, we've been given unique exposure to profound, Eastern ways of looking at the world. I think that's part of what draws us into training. I'm so glad to have you here to talk about the links between Eastern and Western philosophies.

Would you give us a brief look at what motivated you to begin training in the martial arts and a sense of how and when you began to realize the martial arts were your path?

Arthur: What I'm going to say is going to sound familiar to you because, while it feels quite personal to me, it isn't a particularly unique story. First, I have to point out that I was born with a questing gene. From a very early age, and to the consternation of my parents, I had a very dim view of conformity and was very skeptical about how the world worked and the values people ought to espouse. I took a similarly jaundiced view of the standard path of career, job, work, and study that everyone around me seemed to take for granted. In short, you could say I was very suspicious, and not very accepting, about the lens through which most Americans, particularly in the 1970s, understood such things.

I started looking for answers to life's deeper questions early. At the age of 10 or 12, I was already reading Zen koans and Lao Tze's *Tao Te Ching*, along with Buddhist books and works of Western philosophy by the likes of Bertrand Russell and Immanuel Kant. Such material is hard enough to understand now—Lao Tze's little book in particular remains an opaque, though exhilarating, mystical mystery—so I'm sure that despite being a precocious reader I comprehended relatively little of what I read. Still, the point is, I had the urge to try.

I looked to the East for a different worldview because I suffered a lot, both emotionally and physically. My gnawing skepticism about the life I was living took a deep toll, because I pretended, even strove, to fit in. This was in part because of my emotional state as I endured a terrible lung disease. My immune system took a battering from noxious drugs and procedures that would seem positively medieval today, and I spent quite a bit of time just trying to get one more breath and stay alive. While other kids were out playing ball and developing physical strength, conditioning, and hand-to-eye coordination, I was stuck on the sidelines—if I made it to school at all—and I was always the last one to be chosen for any team. On the bright side, though, I did have plenty of time to think and read. Looking at how kids spend their time today, I consider that to have been a real gift.

When I got a little older, I had a couple of grim experiences while traveling around the world. The first experience took place after I won an academic award that led me to a zoological expedition in Paraguay. I ended up out in the jungle with guys who didn't take kindly to people from my religious and socio-economic background. Terrible, abusive things happened in the bush, and it required all of my courage and wits to survive.

Later, when I was only 22 years old and just out of college, I interceded on behalf of a young lady when she was accosted by a drunken policeman on the street in Quito, Ecuador. All I could do was shove the guy away from her. Had I been more martially effective, he would have stayed down and none of the awful, Midnight-Express-like consequences would have unfolded.

Tim: Wow!

Arthur: It was unpleasant, to say the least. At one point, while running from military policemen dressed in hip boots and carrying swagger sticks like Nazi storm troopers, I promised God that if He got me out of the situation alive, I would learn how to protect myself and others more effectively.

When I did manage to get out of jail and get back to the United States, the very first thing I did was go find a class.

Tim: Which martial art did you turn to first?

Arthur: Back then, there were few choices in the small California town in which I attended graduate school. I found a Korean Tang Soo Do school run by David Jang. I have not heard of him in years, but at the time, he was very athletically gifted. I loved to watch him fly through the air over the heads of 5 or 6 people and land a sidekick on a bag with a resounding thud.

His brand of martial arts represented a pure physicality I could not imagine back then, being barely able to touch my toes and having very poor wind as well. Unfortunately, his strict, traditional teaching style—forced stretches and the like—did not match my rebellious, creative spirit. As wonderful as the Korean arts can be, at that time the fit was not good for me so I didn't stay with the training for very long.

Tim: At what point did you find tai chi and begin on that path?

Arthur: The first time I tried tai chi was in San Diego in the early 1980s. It was so painfully slow and difficult, I remember nearly crying from frustration. I just could not sense anything going on. I was still looking at things from a very application-oriented point of view and tai chi's qualities were just too vague and ineffable. It would be some years before I returned to the art. In between, I studied quite a few other martial systems. I'm afraid my experience tree is obnoxiously and pathetically long.

Tim: [laughs]

Arthur: It is tempting to say that it took me a while to find the right thing, but it is probably more accurate to say that the different arts I studied were all part of the journey, and each one was just right for me at the time I engaged in it. People say that when the student is ready the teacher will come; I suppose the same could be said about martial arts systems. All together, the various black belts I garnered and the years spent with different teachers led me to whatever understanding I have today.

I had a great time studying Wing Chun with Calasanz Martinez in the lineage of Moy Yat, a kung fu brother and contemporary of Bruce Lee. I also did some Choy Li Fut, some White Crane Kung Fu while at graduate school at Cornell, and I managed to squeeze in some Shorin Ryu weapons study as well. Then I got some years in and one or two black belts in Ed

Parker's brand of American Kenpo. I liked the functional, street orientation of that art.

About 22 years ago in Los Angeles, I turned to Hsing-i ch'uan and studied with Stuart Charno, a senior student of New York Grandmaster Kenny Gong. That first exposure to the internal arts was a real eye-opener for me, refocusing my attention on energy, relaxation, flexibility, and sensitivity—all ideas I had been exposed to earlier in tai chi, but not at a time when I was receptive to them.

When I did come back to tai chi it was to the Dong family version of Yang style, and then, finally, the time was right. In much the way I observe in new students now, I grew quickly intoxicated by the elegance and beauty of the art and almost immediately gave up all other practices in order to focus on it.

These days the students who come to me seem to have their pump primed to learn the art. This is likely the result of where we are in history. Regardless of the cycles of politics and the economy, the overall trend is away from speed and greed of our materially-driven culture and toward greater environmental sensitivity, and

17

the higher levels of consciousness and compassion inherent in a non-dual philosophy like Taoism, the conceptual parent of tai chi. No doubt the high stress levels we all experience, combined with the increasing cost of health care are contributing to the explosion of interest in tai chi, which we now see in print ads, television programs, and, of course, as the darling of integrative medicine.

A lot of people who come to tai chi do not even know that it is a martial art. That was not the case for me. After my exposure to Hsing-I ch'uan, I was hooked on the idea of accomplishing more with less, of reaching health and martial goals alike with greater focus and efficiency. As I am sure you hear all the time, my preference changed as I got older and wiser and I was less willing to tear down my body and cause injuries that would plague or limit me later in life. I was looking for a softer, more sophisticated, and more fluid martial art.

I live in Florida and sometimes I go down to Key West, which is quite a party scene. Occasionally, I come across people walking down the street wearing a t-shirt that says, "The liver is evil and should be punished." That sort of drinker mentality reminds me of the desire some martial artists have to push the body to harden and strengthen it—to beat it to a pulp if necessary. I remember training in Wing Chun and smashing into that wooden dummy—a piece of Chinese oak—two or three thousand times a night. I punched it with my hands until my knuckles were all swollen and bleeding and the teacher encouraged that stuff. That was good, very macho; it made the hands strong. But, it is not the tai chi way, which is about consistent, moderate practice and the kind of slow, steady gains that not only build the body but deepen the mind.

Tim: So, the second time you took on tai chi you realized some things you had missed the first time?

Arthur: In a sense, it was like trying a diet. We often know that something is good for us or even is *the* thing for us, but we can't quite get to it. I think we could say this about human behavior in a lot of different dimensions. We could say it about people in the way they eat. We could say it about people in the way they behave around money. We could say it about people in the way they acquire material things.

Knowing what is good for us and doing that thing are not one and the same. It often takes just the right confluence of variables to line up to provide that perfect motivational storm.

What finally did it for me was the realization of the precise way in which tai chi differs from every other martial art in the world, whether it is boxing, wrestling, grappling, sword fighting, or even shooting. You see, all these systems, no matter how beautiful, august, traditional, gorgeous, or effective they may be, entail a conversation between opponents. The conversation is a give and take: I give you this; you give me that. This back and forth rhythm sets up a certain quality in our training. If we train alone, we have to imagine the martial conversation in order for our movements and techniques to be convincing. If we train with a partner, we necessarily create a rigid, contrived scenario in which we expect our techniques to work. In much the same way you and I have agreed to have an interesting exchange here, this pugilistic process requires a certain implicit cooperation.

Tim: Right.

Arthur: As far as I know, tai chi is the only martial art that disregards this convention entirely. This is a profound distinction I am making here, and it radically defines tai chi's martial dynamic. Rather than working an externally oriented strategy that varies with the situation and the opponent, tai chi requires us to turn our attention inward. Obviously, I'm not saying we ignore our opponent or pay no attention to what's going on, but what I'm trying to get across is that the preoccupation has everything to do with what we call our *wuji* state. I'm sure you've come across that term.

Tim: As I understand it, it is a term meaning "internal stillness?"

Arthur: Yes, it relates to stillness or emptiness, but I want to take a ninety-second detour just to make clear exactly what *wuji* means.

Tim: Please.

Arthur: Wuji is actually a concept that pertains to our understanding of how the known world came into being. In the West, we derive our cosmogony either from science or from religion. Scientifically, we understand the world to have formed at the time of the Big Bang. Only recently has there been much interest in exploring what might have come before that blessed event.

In religious terms, we have the creation account recounted in the Book of Genesis. This reads, more or less, "In the beginning, God created the heavens and the earth." The implication is that there is a timeline involved. There was a point or points in time before the earth and the heavens existed, and there are now points in time where they do. Heaven and earth, by the way, are opposites. They are a pair. One is up and one is down. One is solid and the other etheric.

The Chinese analog to this religious description reads, "From *wuji* came tai chi." In that context, *wuji* implies the cosmic emptiness before the world as we know it came to exist. In Western terms, we could think of it as the mind of God before anything occurred to Him. That world, in the traditional Chinese view, has a binary character just like the one described in Genesis. Rather than call its components earth and heaven though, it is more common to denote them as the polar opposites of yin and yang. Tai chi means the harmonious interplay of opposing forces, and is the dance between yin and yang.

So it turns out that emptiness is a somewhat misleading definition; at least it is incomplete. The word emptiness suggests that there is nothing there, whereas both Eastern and Western models imply something different. The former suggests that everything was primed and ready for the whole of what is to suddenly organize itself into yin and yang. This organization happens as a result of the system itself; it requires no God to occur, it just does. This leads me to translate wuji as "emptiness (or stillness) pregnant with infinite possibility."

The latter, Western model, again, just means that God was there and the mind of God was active but that's all there was. Then, he got this idea...Heaven and Earth! And, because he was God, everything manifested. Either way, we have a binary universe. Tangentially, it is interesting to note that the ancient Chinese Taoist thinkers described this binary property before anyone else. Had the technology existed then, they might even have invented computers.

In martial arts terms, we can now see that wuji means a "bodymind" devoid of a plan but completely ready to respond to anything. When we are in wuji we are not in motion either intellectually or physically, but we are ready for anything. Going back to the idea of tai chi not being a conversation between opponents we can see that, instead, our goal is to concentrate on keeping our wuji state, or wuji alignment, our own personal version of being still but pregnant with infinite possibility. Thus, when an opponent does something to us our goal is not to throw him in the river, not to smash or crack his head, not to break his arm, not to kick his sensitives into the back of his throat, but rather to simply maintain that perfectly aware, balanced, relaxed state. In Chinese medical terms, all of our meridians are opened, the chi is flowing, everything's working just fine and it is right or comfortable or healthy.

Now, if somebody's arm gets broken and they spit teeth in the course of such a correction, that is not our problem.

Tim: Not our problem. Right. [chuckles]

Arthur: It really is important to recognize that nowhere in the interaction I just described was there any intent to harm. That is really interesting because one of the reasons that some fighters do not take tai chi seriously is because they are under the misapprehension that it is purely a defensive art. That is utter nonsense. Actually, it can be the nastiest, most devastating system around. But, in terms of the *principle* underlying the action, it is as I described to you.

Tim: That's an interesting way of looking at it. I want to take a step now and talk about the differences between, Chen-Style tai chi and Yang-Style tai chi. We study a little bit of Yang-Style in my studio and as far as I can tell, it seems that's the most popular branch of tai chi in the United States. Can you tell us a little bit about what the differences are in technique and philosophy between the two styles?

Arthur: This is a relatively straightforward if emotionally charged subject for some people. It shouldn't be. Tai chi, like all other forms of kung fu, has a history, and in that history are events and lineages. These facts are very clear as far back as about 1600. Earlier than that, we get into the realm of legend and opinion as records have been lost or destroyed. There is a big debate about the earliest origins of tai chi, which certainly go back to ancient Taoist traditions.

What we can say for certain is that in the northern Chinese province of Henan in a village known as Chenjiagou (literally, the Chen family ditch), the art we now know as tai chi has been practiced since 1600.

The father of the movements we recognize now as Chen-Style tai chi was a military commander by the name of Chen Wang Ting. Chen based his art on the philosophy of the Taoist sage Lao Tzu's *Tao Te Ching*, incorporated information from indigenous medicines, and conspired with members of the Li family, to whom he was related and who had studied martial arts on the famous Wudang Mountain.

Chen passed his art down to some other notable names in the lineage including Chen Yang Xi and Chen Fa Ke—the most august master of the last generation—who taught in Beijing until his death in 1957. Many people try to build imaginary or real bridges to Chen Fa Ke.

By all accounts, he was a really, really magnificent fighter and practitioner. In my own lineage, Fa Ke taught Chen Zhao Qui, Chen Zhao Qui taught Chen Shuo Li and Chen Shuo Li taught Chen Quanzhong, who was my grandmaster and the teacher of my primary instructor, Master Max Yan.

What does all this have to do with the difference between Yang and Chen tai chi? The answer is that the former arose from the latter. During the last century, a 14th generation Chen family member by the name of Chen Chang Xing broke with tradition and taught a family outsider, a pharmacy worker by the name of Yang Lu Chan. Yang Lu Chan was an apt pupil and very talented in the martial arts.

One version of the events that ensued—I stress, *one* version—is that when Yang left the Chen village, he was told that he must preserve the Chen family's secrets by keeping what he had learned to himself. When he returned to Beijing, however, he wanted to teach for a living. To honor his agreement with his teacher he deliberately removed Chen tai chi's martial core and formed a new style, which he named for his family.

How much of this is true, and whether or not Yang was warned or threatened in some way, are details lost to the mists of time. Certainly, we can say that kung fu families then and now take their secrets very seriously. Yang's new style of tai chi is certainly different from its progenitor. For one thing, it is a lot simpler. The forms are shorter and the movements are larger and less intricate than those in Chen-Style Tai Chi.   Furthermore, Yang style is practiced at a steady cadence, making it less energetically variable than Chen style, which is episodically fast and hard and then is very soft again and slow.

Perhaps most significantly from a martial point of view, Chen style emphasizes a three-dimensional movement, which, in my experience with sparring, pushing and watching, is mostly lost in Yang style. That is not to say that there are not some Yang students who have rediscovered it in their own study of the movements—they figured out what was taken out and sort of organically put it back in.

Anyway, all tai chi people should be grateful to Yang style for being more accessible than Chen style, being beautiful to watch and play, for becoming hugely popular, and for all it has done for millions of people in terms of health and longevity. I and every other Chen stylist who has any character or brains respects the Yang system. Our perspective is just that it's a simplified version of what we do.

Tim: I see, and it's wonderful to hear about the legends, as you say, but obviously none of us were there, so it's hard to verify these types of stories.

Arthur: I know. I love the legends, but, in the end, it doesn't really matter whether they are true; what matters is that they inspire and educate us. We imbue them with the qualities that we're looking for that are important to help us understand and remember.

Tim: It's good to hear the stories of the past and how these styles developed into what they are today. With regard to your more recent lineage and in bringing Chinese styles and Chinese philosophies over to the West, what do you think has really developed and how have things changed and evolved in our more recent history? What's been added to styles? What may have been lost from these styles, and how do you think tai chi has been evolving recently?

Arthur: Tai chi is built on a tripod. One leg is traditional Chinese medicine and the energetics pertaining thereto. Another leg is the long history of body mechanics that come from the folk martial arts of China, the organic, on-the-dusty-road techniques that either worked or didn't. Those that didn't were abandoned or lost.

The third leg, of course, is Taoist philosophy. I think it's a fair statement that nowhere is there a system of movement that is more intimately interdigitated, more intimately and perfectly expressive of a system of philosophy than Chen-Style Tai Chi is of Lao Tzu's brand of philosophical Taoism. Speaking of Lao Tzu, if the great sage heard the question you asked me about what has been lost or how tai chi is evolving, and heard my sadness about the way things have changed in China and what has happened to these magnificent arts, I'm sure he would caution me, in a curiously Buddhist way, against my attachment to the old way of things. He would laugh and say, "You know, this is the way of things, the way of water. It's the cycle of nature that things are born and then they die and that they change and become something else."

The relevance of internal martial arts to longevity is arguably less in the modern West than it is in the ancient East, because we have all these pharmaceuticals and we have all the medical technologies that prolong our life. Now, those of us who have experience with these things know that it's better not to go there because in every pill there's a little poison. Procedures and such are fallible, dangerous and expensive; it's always better to prevent than to cure.

On the surface, the link between internal practice and longevity seems less important to most people these days because it's easier to call a doctor and take a pill than it is to get up and work out. Of course, on a deeper level, any longevity practice seems to me more proactive and preventative than curative, and the benefits of practice still outweigh those of scrambling around to fix what you have let happen to you out of laziness, poor decisions, or ennui. Tai chi is self-defense against the degenerative diseases of lifestyle and aging.

In a further answer to your question, there are changes in the role of tai chi as traditional self-defense as well. I live in Florida, where getting a concealed weapon permit is easy enough and every grandma has a revolver in her glove box. So, the relevance of being able to take care of yourself physically today in the United States, compared to the importance of these skills in historical China where infrastructure was absent and physical threats were constant and real is obviously also different. We live in a gun culture.

As far as the mind and body go, there is a definite hunger for the practice. I see it every day. I feel it in myself and I see it in my students. The hunger arises from the consequences of living in that speed and greed world we talked about earlier. There's a deep, quiet, abiding place in all of us that wants not to be involved in what we call the "rat race" or to feel what we call the stresses of modern life. Tai chi practice provides a refuge from those stresses, and that is something new and different that might have been less true hundreds of years ago in China.

As far as any evolving interest in Taoist philosophy, I think there's a strong trend toward Eastern ways of looking at things, especially since Ralph Waldo Emerson's contribution. That is because we are a young and inexperienced country and the only real indigenous wisdom here was shot, chopped, and butchered as we spread across the land and erased the Native American population. I think the spiritual bankruptcy of mainstream American culture has left many of us feeling disenfranchised. We crave feeling that we are part of something, which is why there is a movement toward non-dual philosophies that bring everything together as one experience and manifestation as opposed to many separate and unrelated phenomena.

You can find evidence of interest in Taoist philosophy by looking at the vast number of English translations of Lao Tzu's *Tao Te Ching*, the philosophical bible of tai chi practice. There are 50 or 60 translations. I have many of them on my bookshelf.

By the way, Taoist ideas pervade our popular culture, although people may not recognize them for what they are. The *Star Wars* series is a great example of this. George Lucas was a great devotee of Lao Tzu and everything his film project spawned— including cartoons, action figures, and so on—is rife with Taoism. The Jedi knights are tai chi masters defending nature. Venerating nature is a Taoist theme, and Lucas' take on it, which casts inorganic, high-tech bad guys against fuzzy, natural beings like the Ewoks and the Wookies, brings Taoist ideas to the modern mainstream.

Lucas isn't Taoism's only proponent. James Cameron really got into it with *Avatar* in a big way, and *Star Trek* involves Taoist themes too. So does the California surf culture which exhorts us to go with the flow. All of these popular ideas came from the same intellectual roots as tai chi.

Tim: The people I speak to and my perspective on the arts tells me that people are beginning to turn to these philosophies for both creative abstraction and for solutions to the problems we're facing, whether in medicine or elsewhere.

Arthur: Definitely. We are biological beings. You can change the external environment all you want, but certain facts remain: we're still creatures of gristle, muscle, neuron, bone and blood. We work a certain way and we respond a certain way and that was as true in the time of Chen Wang Ting as it is today. We are also spiritual beings, which means we hunger for a sense of meaning and purpose as well. We want abstract context and connection from our mind/body practices and we want practical results too. We want these practices to teach us how to deal with life better, to manage our emotion and our health and our wellness. The good news is that tai chi can do all that. If it could not and did not, it would have been lost to things that worked better, again, on that dusty road in China way back when.

Speaking of the dusty road and things that work, I want to bring up a pet subject here. It is one I feel strongly about, namely the role of weapons training in tai chi.

There are many people who do not know that tai chi is a martial art, and an even greater number who do not know, despite having seen players swing a wooden sword around, that tai chi is a battlefield system that arose from the use of weapons. Before there were open-hand techniques and forms, tai chi was all about traditional Chinese weapons.

It is always surprising to me how few practitioners of tai chi are aware of the deep level of information about the proper, efficient, and effective use of weapons that exists in all the tai chi forms, including those long sets designed for empty-handed practice. A really good example of this is the Chen-Style Tai Chi long form. That form, which we call *Lao Da Jia* (meaning old, large frame) contains between 80 and 240 movements, depending upon how you break it up and count. It is one of the longest and most complex forms in any style of Chinese martial arts.

I mention it here because what most folks don't know—and this is going to startle some people—is that it derives largely from a weapon called the *Guan Dao* (also known as the Spring and Autumn Broadsword or Chinese Halberd). It's a big weapon with a five-foot shaft, spear point on one end, and a hooked and wickedly pointed two-foot blade on the other end.

When Chen Wang Ting concocted what we now know as the progenitor of all the tai chi open-handed forms, he did so drawing directly from the movements and requirements of that mighty weapon wielded on horseback in war. To understand at least some of those requirements, you have to think about the metallurgy back then. Weapons manufacture was not nearly what it is today. The big halberd was a heavy, clumsy sword made of wrought iron and wood. It was wielded by folks who were not, for the most part, as large or well-nourished as we Americans are. They rode bareback, holding onto the horse with their knees, the reins in one hand, and the sword in the other. Imagine trying to swing around a weapon like that and have it come into contact with something like a head, a sword, a leg, a torso, or armor. Simply to not be unhorsed by the momentum of your own forward progress plus the swing of the weapon was a feat requiring tremendous technique and incredible strength.

If you were here with me, Tim, and you could see how I mimic the riding and halberd-wielding position, you would smile, nod, and immediately recognize the tai chi horse stance. You would see how the knees and the femur inwardly rotate to open the hip joint. You would

37

see the way the weapon is held and twisted and turned and the way the waist controls it. You would see how all the joints extend and open and turn and move so that impact doesn't break bones or tear muscles. All these tai chi qualities, which we could talk about together for hours, come directly from the requirements of the practical, nitty-gritty war setting.

I got onto this riff because you asked me about what people might be looking for in their practice. In that connection, I think it's important to understand that despite tai chi's association with the New Age movement and its occasional grouping with yoga, and despite the fact that it can be a wonderful method for artistic self-expression for many people, at its heart, tai chi is a very practical system. It was more heavily influenced—indeed conceived— not by hard-drinking, sex-loving, meditating hermits in mountain caves but by warriors who developed it to accomplish very specific martial goals. All those folks who view the art as moving meditation have no idea of the existence of the halberd from which the art springs.

I would go one step further and say that if a tai chi player is not familiar with the Guan Dao and does not understand its role in the shape and workings of the art, he or she is missing something important in terms of understanding the derivation of the practice and its details and meaning.

Tim: So you're saying that practicing with this large weapon is valuable because it exaggerates what we are doing right and wrong and helps us refine tai chi body mechanics.

Arthur: Exactly. The movements that we do without the weapon, and all the body mechanics that we apply to the shorter weapons come down to the basic broad strokes that were laid down for the Guan Dao. I emphasize this to give you an example of how much of the original intent and content of the art has been lost. The average middle-aged person practicing tai chi in the park to feel better from their arthritis, asthma, depression, chronic fatigue or whatever else, would never know that everything he or she is doing started out with the management of a giant, wicked-looking sword while on horseback.

Tim: Do you think that way back when tai chi was first being developed there was any emphasis on the health benefits, or was it all just a combat style?

Arthur: All I can do is speculate. My best guess is that once the proven martial qualities of the art brought more practitioners into the fold, observers began to notice a few things.

Number one, these hypothetical observers noticed that tai chi players were good fighters who went to war and came home. This was no small thing. Battles were bloody, ferocious, and devoid of evac helicopters and the like. If you were badly wounded, the likelihood was you died. Surviving using tai chi skills was a great testament to the art's effectiveness in the life-or-death proposition called battle and a sign that Chen tai chi players could handle practitioners of other arts.

Remember, infrastructure was nearly absent and the Chen village was a little village in a rural hinterland. There were plenty of bandits and assassins around. Good tai chi fighters were hired as mercenaries, which was good work back in the day, whether the client was an official, a rich man, or an emperor, and our imaginary observer would have noticed that the art thus provided not only survival but a good living.

The art was better suited to armed conflict and multiple opponents than it was to street violence. Of course, the preeminence of the Guan Dao in tai chi history is not the whole story. Other weapons came into play, including the curved saber or Dao, a weapon much like a machete and equally accessible to people who had no special martial arts training—precisely the reason it was so popular—a sword with conscripted farmers and the like. Later, the two-handed, heavy, battlefield straight sword evolved into a smaller, thinner, lighter, and more agile weapon appreciated by scholars for its nimble, elegant look and feel, and adopted by gentlemen of the leisure class because it could easily be carried under a robe for protection. All these details, of course, illustrate tai chi's practicality. By the way, I am personally very fortunate to have been taught the art by members of a generation who survived using tai chi in the era of the gun and survived.

Tim: Wow!

Arthur: Wow is right, and I think about this a lot. But, let's get back to the longevity and health question you asked me. In addition to noticing that tai chi worked in battle and brought home the bacon as a mercenary practice, I have to believe that those practitioners who did not die in battle evidenced good health and a long life. I'm sure people noticed this, and a logical assumption is that even non-warriors began to practice the forms and solo exercises, knowing that the skills they were developing not only might save their life someday in an altercation, but they would also contribute to a long life.

Tim: Growing up in a Western culture, it seems we have very well-defined ideas and principles that make introspective Eastern ideas a bit hard to access. What are your thoughts on how we can better expose people, including our youth, to healthy, Eastern alternatives in general, and to tai chi practice and philosophy in particular?

Arthur: That is a big question. Admiring our country's founding spirit and loving the freedoms and luxuries and choices many of us enjoy does not stop me from seeing the social, environmental, educational, and financial mistakes we are making and the problems those mistakes engender. When you have spent decades studying traditional Chinese philosophy and culture, it is easy to have a less-than-enthusiastic view of many of the assumptions and prejudices we have in the United States.

This is a large conversation, and one that goes on out there in the media all day, every day, 24/7. It is a conversation about our children, the diminution in attention span that comes with the tools of the digital age, the change in values that comes from a disconnection from the natural world and from each other—at least in terms of skin-to-skin opportunities and what many have come to call *face time*—and the shifting notions we have about community and mutual respect.

In defense of our anti-culture, let me say that we are a very young country. The only problem is that we're going to have to adapt and grow and learn at an unprecedented rate because we've reached a sort of biological threshold on the planet. Resources are dwindling and the human species is growing with parasitic speed and in cancer-like fashion.

43

We have no choice but to change this if we are to survive, and it's anybody's guess whether we'll succeed. The good news is that necessity is the mother of invention, and we sure have necessity. I am most emphatically *not* someone who believes that technology has all the answers, though using our old, problematic systems in new ways may buy us some time. Rather, I believe that we're better off looking to ethics, morals, and evolution for solutions. I say evolution because the brain is an organ and responds to the pressures of natural selection, as does any other. As our situation becomes more and more dire, our survival will be in question. As that time approaches, the evolutionary forces at work on us will increase. What I hope happens, and what some say is already happening, is that we will experience an evolutionary leap in consciousness—possible, if you believe that consciousness is a property of mind and brain—that will have us seeing each other and the world differently. The result of that will be a necessary change in the way we behave, consume, pollute, make war, and so on.

I hope it is not too late for that. In the meantime, as I said, technology offers some solutions. Among these is better and more widespread communications using the internet, films, books, TV, and more. As it happens, I have a television show running nationally on PBS right now and for another couple of years or so. It is titled *Longevity Tai Chi*. It is more of a "why to" than a "how to" show, because it is so hard to teach or learn tai chi without a teacher present. Done in documentary fashion, the show demonstrates compelling scientific evidence for the benefits the art brings. There is some very cool footage on that show.

In one instance, for example, I'm in the lab of a researcher named Dr. Shin Lin who was coincidentally a Chen style practitioner who studied under one of my ancillary teachers, Chen Zhenglei. In his laboratory at the University of California at Irvine, you can see Dr. Lin using a very high-tech device to evaluate the emission of photons from Lao Gong, an acupuncture point in the center of my palm. Before I practice tai chi, there are no photons. After practicing just a few minutes of tai chi, photons—light energy—stream from my palm. No Jedi mind trick this, but real science.

Tim: [laughs]

Arthur: There are other cool things too, like a spike in electricity across the surface of the skin after practice. It's all very cutting edge.

Tim: And you have written some books on the topic as well, is that right?

Arthur: Interestingly, although I am the author of 11 published books it has taken me a long time to get around to writing a book about tai chi. That's because I have always figured the longer I wait the more I will know, and of course because I've had some reservations about trying to teach such a challenging art form using a book. What I've come to realize, at last, is that I can do with the book what I did with the TV show, namely to argue, in what I hope is a convincing fashion, for tai chi's important role in the modern world. The book that does this is called *Tai Chi — The Perfect Exercise* and it is due out in April 2013.

I have some other books out there that engage themes of Chinese history and philosophy in an entertaining fashion: one is called *The Crocodile and the Crane*, an apocalyptic novel that pops back and forth in time. The protagonists are brother and sister Taoist immortals who have lived for thousands of years and seen everything there is to see.

In addition to a best-selling non-fiction book titled *The Truth About Chronic Pain,* I also have a fun series of thrillers featuring a neurosurgeon who works for a hospital in South Florida and goes out at night as a vigilante with a sword. [chuckles]

Tim: [chuckles]

Arthur: Beyond my books, I have a website, www.playtaichi.com and a blog on *The Huffington Post.* I do some book reviews there, but mostly I try to bring my acquired Eastern perspective to the Western world. I also have a few short films on YouTube.

Tim: That's great. I've watched a lot of your videos and they're very entertaining. As you said, you come at it from a scientific standpoint a lot of the time, which I think is great—being both an engineer and a Westerner, I think that you provide a good easy-to-understand perspective for a lot of people.

Thank you. I could probably talk to you for another couple of hours about all this stuff. It's been fascinating, and I really appreciate it. But, I will let you go and say thank you so much for sharing your wisdom with all of us.

Arthur: My pleasure, and thank you for all the good you're doing with your project.

Brought to you by

Find the audio version of this interview at:

www.MALineage.com/episode19

About the Martial Arts Lineage Project

The Martial Arts Lineage Project works to document the lineage of all styles of martial arts worldwide and preserve the history and legacy of martial arts legends of the past and present.

We are all connected through the flowing river of martial arts lineage that links instructors to students, generation after generation. The lessons learned by one generation are passed on to the next in a never-ending cycle of sharing and learning.

Imagine if we could see back in time to the ancient masters who developed these arts as tools for survival, daily empowerment, the enrichment of life, and a better human race. To understand *anything* it is best to learn it first-hand from the source. We bring you interviews and discussions with legendary martial artists from across the country and around the world. Authors, instructors, and anthropologists share their insights on the world of martial arts to give you a better perspective of what is out there and where it all comes from.

Come visit the Martial Arts Lineage Project online to get a glimpse into the past and become a part of the massive interactive tree of martial arts lineage. Create your own interactive lineage tree, share stories about your instructors and your favorite quotes that have motivated you all these years to keep training harder. Watch videos and look at pictures of martial artists of years past to understand what your style was like long before you were born.

To look into the face and hear the words of someone so legendary, so powerful, and so influential is inspiring and insightful.

每一代人
将收获
播种前一代。

Each generation will reap
what the former generation
has sown.

Become part of the Lineage Project today at:

www.MALineage.com

Printed in Great Britain
by Amazon